A Memoir

Beyond Me
Reflections, Poems and Love Letters

Shanita Jackson

Beyond Me: Reflections, Poems and Love Letters

Editor: Elijah Jean Editing

DEDICATION

To my grandmothers, Roxie Lee Williams and Jean Mae Watts. Two women filled with wisdom. They gave me the foundation I needed to endure life. They developed the foundation of my faith and for that, I am forever grateful. Truly, my first best friends; I miss you both.

To my mother, who has always been my supporter. I love you always.

To my dear friend, Shanique Baker. Because of you, I cherish friendships all the more. You were the true definition of a friend. I love you and miss you forever. April 12, 2018, changed my life forever. I know how much you loved books, so I dedicate this to you.

To my family, friends and mentors, who have all played a part collectively to help me throughout my journey. Thank you to each and every one of you.

PREFACE

This journey called life is about conquering. There was a time I felt as if the people that entered my world, interrupted and invaded my story without my permission. Through this book, I share some of the experiences and lessons I have learned throughout my journey. I hope that my story empowers you and helps you to move forward through your journey. May the words throughout the pages appear to walk off the page and become reality where you too are ready to walk out your journey.

Now, that I am strong, I take back what is rightfully mine and give you my story without interruptions.

FOREWORD

This is not your ordinary book. I bet you are thinking, "that's an unusual way to begin a foreword". You are correct, and that's because this isn't your typical book. Shanita's writing style and passion is peculiarly special.

She unashamedly dives into her past with hopes of pulling readers out of their miserable misfortune. Her descriptive demonstration of despair and despondency will be HOPE to her generation.

As you journey through these pages, you will discover a life on paper. Something of a nonfictional storyline to amuse you. I must warn you that it may sound like a movie script. Before you drift off with imagination, remember this is her life and story. This will take you beyond her, beyond them and in the words of S. J. Jackson, "This is Beyond Me!"

Dr. Jerry D. Owens

BEYOND ME

ROXIE'S GIRL

My Grandma was not too thrilled that her daughter was pregnant. In her defense, what would a sixteen-year-old do with a child? Grandma didn't want her child to have a baby so she took my mom to the clinic. Abortion wasn't a word my mom quite understood; the definition she knew, but the thought of her getting rid of something she helped to create was foreign. "I'm keeping it," she said with as much authority a sixteen-year-old could to their mother. The imprint of my grandmother's hand left on my mother's face was traced with fear. Nine months later the memory of it disappeared and I would become "Roxie's girl."

***

The year 1995 was the beginning of my story. I was sitting in my Kindergarten class when I heard the office secretary voice over the intercom.

"Ms. B, please send Shanita Jackson to the front office to go home."

I gathered my things and the class hall monitor escorted me out. She asked if everything was ok and I told her I thought so. I wasn't sure why I was going home but I didn't complain. It felt nice to be going home early, yet, when we got to the office confusion set in.

"Where's my mom? Where's my grandma?" I said to no one specifically. I didn't know who would have the answer but I knew someone in this office full of adults had to know something. I searched for a familiar face to tell me what was going on but instead was met by a stranger.

"You're going with me, Shanita. I'm from Health and Rehabilitative Services (HRS), but don't worry you're in good hands."

Her hand extended out to greet mine and her attempted smile tried to soften the blow of this news but it didn't help. My mom always told me not to trust strangers and this one was no different. She was a stranger and there was no way I would be leaving with her.

During the car ride, I remained quiet, but my thoughts raced. *Where am I going? Why did she pick me up? Where are my siblings? Is she taking me to my mom?* I wanted answers, but I refused to talk to the lady. She asked me questions about myself yet, they all fell on deaf ears. My face fell into the palms of my hands and tears blurred my eyes. She said it would be okay but I didn't believe her.

I felt the car stop and uncovered my eyes to a plain, white, tall building with lots of windows. Once inside, I was relieved to see my siblings. From this moment, things moved rather quickly. I went from consoling my siblings to seeing my mom and grandma walk through the door. While they went to talk with the social worker, I stayed with my siblings. After what seemed like hours, the social worker walked in and told us to gather our belongings to go home with my grandma.

Being in the arms of my grandma was comforting. She was the type of woman to say whatever was on her mind. Although she was stern, she was loving. She would cut up cantaloupe and fix my favorite foods just for me. I remember spending a lot of time with her. Her home was filled with a lot of "what-nots" and prayer. Every day my grandma would wake up at 5 am to pray with her friends on the prayer line. Her consistency led me to believe that prayer had to be a part of my daily life. As I continued to get older, I would hear my grandma talk about God and pray with and for her friends which is what led me to develop my own faith.

There would be times I would go to her for prayer and scriptures I couldn't seem to find. Little did I know the lessons I learned from my grandma would be lessons I would soon use with my siblings being back in the care of my mom.

***

Bam Bam Bam.

I heard a knock at the door. I wondered if it was my grandma coming back from work early.

My mom answered the knock and a familiar voice greeted her. It was the social worker here for her routine check-in. The sight of her meant that this would end badly. My grandmother wasn't home and my mom was only allotted supervised visits, yet, here we were, unsupervised with her.

Before we knew it, we were back to the social worker's office. I'm not sure of all the details in between; however, I clearly remember the ride to the group home. My sister, Bre, and I went to the group home together while my younger three siblings went to a different placement home.

When we arrived, we entered the group home with several other children. The social worker spoke with the staff and introduced us before signing paperwork and leading us to our rooms. My sister and I had separate rooms. The room that I would be sleeping in was shared with two other girls. The staff pointed to the bunk bed on the bottom and introduced me to my roommates then left us alone to get settled in.

I cried all night. I was scared and unsure of the unknown. The only time I stayed away from home was to sleep over at family's house; here there was no family. I was nervous to share a room with strangers and I could not understand why Bre couldn't sleep in the room with me. I just wanted to go home. I wished my Grandma was home when the social worker came by the house. This was all one big nightmare that I wanted to wake up from.

The next day, my social worker came to visit Bre and I. I was so happy to see a familiar face. "I have good news, " she said. "I found a foster parent that is willing to take you and all four of your siblings." It was the best news I heard all day. I would finally be reunited with all my siblings. With the biggest smile plastered on my face, I packed my belongings and headed out the door unaware of the life that lay ahead.

***

As the years went by, it seemed my childhood went quickly with it. We stayed with our foster mother for about a year. She was physically abusive but the thought of being separated from my siblings was worse. I just wanted to be a kid and prayed for a moment of peace. School became my solace so I excelled at it. I would go above and beyond to take on the role of the "line leader"—the first in line to lead the class to our next destination. I upheld this job as if my life depended on it. It was a position I knew well because I had the same job at home. While mom went to work or made a quick errand to the store I was the line leader of my siblings. I was always the leader. Whenever my mom had to work late and was not able to cook dinner, I had the responsibility to make dinner, help with homework and bath time. I can still hear my mother telling me to get the hamburger meat, spaghetti sauce and noodles.

I became my mother's significant other, and the second parent to my siblings. We were all we had. I wanted the wealthy parents that could afford to fly me around the world. Little did I know we were in poverty. Blind to the fact, I was under the impression that receiving food stamps and section-8 was a normal thing for black families. It wasn't until I entered my teenage years I understood we were struggling.

I must admit there was a time I blamed my mother for not being able to be like my friend's mom or my teachers' that took me under their wings. I did not quite understand what was going on with my mother or what she was going through. She worked long hours to ensure that my siblings and I were fed because she had no help. My father was not around because he was deported back to the Bahamas when I was two-years-old leaving my teenage mother to raise me alone. Despite my home life, I worked hard to be a great kid. I hid behind my books and schoolwork and stayed focus on my education. The adult me applauds my mom because she played with the cards that she was dealt. No matter what she had my back. I could talk to her about anything and she wouldn't judge me. She listened and allowed my voice to be heard and if I ever was out of line she made sure to correct me. "Shanita, be better than me," a piece of advice she always gave that I kept close to my heart.

I loved her and I knew she loved me, even if I did not hear her say it much. She showed it through her playful ways even when I thought she was aggravating. She showed her love by going to work day after day to make ends meet and ensure that my siblings and I had food to eat, a roof to live under and clothes to wear. I knew we had a bond, but as a young girl I really could not put the words together to explain my relationship with my Mom. What I did not understand as a child, I understand now. When my Mom had options as a sixteen-year-old, she decided to give birth to me. Through it all, she found the strength to hold it together the best way she knew how to hold it together. Despite our shortcomings, we both pushed through and when it seemed my back was against the wall I used education as my outlet. For a while, my grades reflected this; yet, as more time passed on and more responsibility piled up my grades began to drop and my behavior fell with them.

***

In sixth grade, I was suspended from school for insubordination for hitting a boy in the head with a book. It was the first time and I vowed to make it the last. When I arrived home that day, I checked the mail and found the referral my teacher sent home. Not wanting my mom to see it, I hid it from her, scared for what she would say and do. I never been in trouble or reprimanded and I did not want to start. I always followed the rules at home and school so I knew there was no way I could explain the suspension. I witnessed my siblings getting spanked for acting out at school and I did not want to be hit. So, for me, it was better to behave and follow what was being asked of me.

In school, many of the kids would play a game called flipping. It was our version of gambling and although I tried to avoid it the thought of winning money so easily became more enticing. I was intrigued and wanted to know what this game was all about.

"Do you want in?" one of my classmates asked one day as I stood back and watched. I knew I couldn't pass this opportunity up and if I was going to play I wanted to be the best.

"How do you play?" I asked.

"All you need is some change, a quarter, nickel or dime, then you pick who goes first. The other player has to match the first person to win, if not then the other person wins."

It sounded too easy to be true, And I knew if I did this I'll be able to have money for the snack bar and I could help save my Mom some money. It was a win-win situation.

"I'm in."

I flipped and kept on flipping and before I knew it I was up three dollars. I was hooked. Flipping became my everyday school hustle and as time went by, I stopped asking my Mom for money in the mornings. Whatever she would have given me, I knew I could make that in a game.

By the time I became a seventh grader, flipping became part of my daily ritual. I was officially a gambler. I needed money to buy snacks from the snack bar because I was not a fan of the school lunch. My mom was not aware that I was gambling even though I often asked her for her change; whether it be a quarter, a nickel or a dime. She would never ask me why I needed it. But she would give it to me right before she dropped me off on the corner of the school. She always offered to take me to the front door but I would refuse. The four-door dusty blue car had rust in several spots. I did not want my friends to see that we drove such an ugly, beat up car.

During my high school years, we moved a lot. We lived in section-8 housing and was always moving to find a better home in a better community. I never really asked questions. When the time came, I'd pack my room and help pack the house and just like that we would be on to the next location. For the first week of ninth grade, I went to Evans High School in Orlando, Florida. We moved to a new house and I finished the year out at Oakridge High School. I enjoyed Oakridge because I was involved in JROTC. Every Wednesday I would put on my uniform and wear it proud. It felt like

I belonged to something. Yet the moment didn't last for long because in tenth grade, we moved again. My sophomore and the rest of my high school experience took place at Agape School. At first, I didn't like Agape because I was bullied most of my tenth-grade year because some of the upperclassmen questioned me about my sexuality. I was sitting on the staircase when Dee—one of my classmates—came outside to ask me if I was gay. I knew he was pushed up to ask me especially because I always hung out with the boys. They took me under their wings like their little sister. I felt comfortable with the guys because they did not dwell on if I had a boyfriend, who I was having sex with or if I wasn't having sex. I could talk about sports and have intellectual conversations with them. I was able to be myself. Over time, as they got to know me and vice versa being at Agape became a more enjoyable experience. I became heavily involved in school activities. I began volunteering in the elementary classes, I was an assistant in the front office, I joined the choir, played basketball, I was a scorekeeper and then the senior class president. Things finally started to turn around and it seemed the hurt little girl was finally finding her peace.

<u>LETTERS TO AL</u>

Dear Al,

I wrote you a letter and put all the change I saved up for you in an envelope. To my surprise, I received the letter back without the change. The envelope had been ripped. The tears begin to flow. My heart was broken. I put everything in the envelope that I had in my piggy bank. I don't know when I'll be able to save up that much again. Oh well, maybe it won't be long before we get to meet in person.

Love Always,

Shanita

Dear Al,

You were deported when I was two years old. I have no memories with you—you left before I could. I wanted you to be around. I would dream of the day you would come around, not sure whether I would call you Dad or Al. Being around your mom, Mima and extended family members, all I heard was "Gina, she looks every spit of Al." I wanted to be daddy's little princess.

Al, why couldn't you be like your sister? She went to college and became successful. You guys were raised in the same household. *Geesh.* You didn't have to be exactly like your sister, but you could've used her as a fuel for motivation. I believe you would not have been deported if you could have got yourself together.

Until next time,

Shanita

Dear Al,

The first time I met you, I was eleven-years-old. I was afraid to reach out to hug you because of the unknown. In my eyes, you were a stranger. I did not know you even though I heard stories about you. My mother never told me much about you, but she ensured me that if you lived in the United States, you would have provided my needs. I wanted to call you 'Dad' out of respect but Al was easier to say. I wanted to be mad at you and never to speak again but I did not fly to your country alone just to return home with no answers.

When I saw you for the first time, I was surprised to see that I looked like you. You have such pretty, white teeth and glowing chocolate skin. Your masculine stance dominated the room. You walked into the house with flowers in your hand and said, "These are for you baby girl." I wanted to be mad at you, never to speak to you again but my heart instantly lit up the moment my eyes landed on your face. It was as if I was looking in the mirror; Grandma was right I look exactly like you.

This hug meant everything to me. Like a little child running into her parent's arms for protection, except that little child was me. Your embrace held all the words I wanted you to say yet never heard. "I am sorry for not being there to raise you. I am sorry for all the time I lost to see you grow." I wanted to stuff you into my suitcase and bring you back to the United States with me but I knew it couldn't happen.

That night, after meeting you, I cried my eyes out because I did not want to leave you. I did not know if that would have been the last time I ever saw you again. And the thought alone was unbearable.

Signed,

Shanita

Dear Al,

The summer of 2004' I went to see Auntie Rochelle and Uncle Keith. This visit brought back so many memories of you. I would watch as Uncle Keith wrapped his daughter into a full embrace and love would fill the room. It took me back to our first encounter only to realize that may have been our last. The way my uncle embraced his daughter put me back into your arms like the first day I met you.

Dad, can you look me into the eyes and I become mesmerized by the love you have for me? Dad, could you tuck me in at night and tell me that you love me? I daydreamed of the days I wanted to spend with you. Where are you? I am fourteen now, time is swiftly moving. I need you like the ocean needs its waves. My rhythm is off without you near. Why did I have to wake up and fast forward to not being able to see you until the day of Mima's funeral?

Talk Later,

Shanita

Dear Al,

It's the summer of 2015 and for the first time, you attempted to have a "birds and the bees" talk. My facial expression showed it all. "I don't want to be rude, but do you think we need to have this talk?" I said. I am 25-years-old. It may be a little late. This is our third time actually seeing each other, make it count. I do not desire for you to speak to me as if I am a child. Ask me about my hobbies. Ask me about my goals in life.

Please, just get to know me.

Shanita

Dear Al,

The hardest part about not growing up with you near is I had to endure all the boy problems alone. I looked for love from the few relationships I was in because I wanted validation and for some insane reason I believed I could be validated by the guy that told me he loved me and wanted to change my last name.

I was afraid to enter relationships because you were not there to be my first example of love. In my current relationship, I've come to realize that I have been missing a major step to move forward and deal with us. Of course, we cannot go back in time. However, we can work on our relationship and connect the puzzle together. You've been the puzzle and I need to add to the masterpiece.

I met you only three times in my entire life. For some reason I still missed you. I never got to know you.

I know you love me; I hear it in your voice in the moments when we are able to converse via phone. I just want to get it right and work towards a better relationship with the man that conceived me. I write you this letter to say, Dad, I love you with my whole heart and I am glad to know you. I was shocked and impressed that you made a conscious decision to make me your one and only child, although you had ample times to add behind me.

Thank you for always respecting me. You always listened when I spoke without interruption even when my words were harsh. You honored me. And although you did not have much money, you made sure to buy a calling card to speak to me. In the moments where we were able to communicate via phone, you ensure that your baby girl is alright. Every year you make the time to call me a day before my birthday to say, "I called early to be the first one to say Happy birthday baby girl." You make my heart melt. I am like you in so many ways. You're compassionate, loving, strong-willed, smart and willing to work through anything to make the best of it.

I love you, Al!

With Love,

Baby girl Shanita

Dear Al,

      Respect, handle with care and be gentle as possible.

Shanita

<u>FORGIVENESS</u>

Writing the letters and journal entries allowed me to flow freely without reservation. Writing gave me peace that although my father was not physically present, he was with me in spirit.

There are always three sides to a story, yours, theirs and the truth. If I had not taken the opportunity to forgive him for not being present, I would have been bound in so many other ways. This by far was one of many steps to my healing process.

<u>UNPRETTY</u>

I am ugly.
No one wants me.
Who am I?
Nobody.
My looks disgust me.
Why was I born this way?
I feel ugly on the inside and it's spilling over,
contaminating the outside.

SILENT BATTLES

My mind races with thoughts and the tears flow
When will I ever get it right?
Will I ever get it right?
Why do I want what I want?
Is it necessary?
I look at my peers and compare myself to them
Why, at times do I feel so inferior to even myself?
I allow distractions and tactics to get the best of me
The battles come and go
Silent battles
It hurts and pierces my soul
I yearn to be better than I was yesterday and the day
before
I don't want to fight this war anymore
I surrender
Silent battles will no longer interfere
Make me sound

LABELS

I defined myself with negative labels. Even when positivity stared me in the face, I fought back with what I felt on the inside. Looking through Teen Magazine or watching various television shows; I would compare my world to theirs.

> *Why wasn't my hair straight or long and curly?*
> *Why was I born with parents that were not wealthy?*
> *Why Me?*

The questions continued to be added to the list. I noticed every label I attached to myself seeped through my pores.

SURVIVOR

I did not have the privilege to be validated by my biological father. My innocence was taken from me at an early age. I was molested by my mother's husband and by the age of 17, I was raped by a guy I met on social media; during that time Myspace was the hot commodity. I felt so ashamed to ever reveal that I was raped. This was all my fault. Why was I stupid to go on a site to meet someone I never knew and allow myself to get in the car with this person. Looking back now, I understand it was not my fault.

It never was.

<u>DADDY ISSUES</u>

Fathers are the first example girls have of love. Our fathers are who we turn to as the blueprint to the attributes of our future spouses, our probable love of our lives.

My father was absent and emotionally unavailable to me. I did not wake up to my father in the mornings before school nor did he tuck me in at night. I began to search for what I perceived to be love and security through intimate relationships. It is then, my issues started unraveling.

After being molested during my childhood and raped at the age of seventeen I longed for my Dad to come rescue me; yet, he was nowhere to be found. Trust became foreign to me. I could not keep a guy around no matter how hard I tried to please him or have sex with him.

When I was treated well I held on to a guy for dear life, even if they weren't good for me. I thought He was different.

He called me his girlfriend, we were together for at least a year and we talked about marriage. He even let me meet some of his family including his father.

Meeting family is a big deal so I knew I had to be *the one*—his future wife. He said I was wife material and he could see himself marrying me. We discussed having children. I thought if I changed the way I dressed to appear to be more girly and fix my hair a certain way and apply some make-up; I would be wanted and He would keep me. I was gullible and naive.

If only I had my daddy to teach me....

CAN I HAVE IT BACK?

Noble stood six feet tall, with such pretty brown eyes, and a nice smile. I thought he was out of my league. There was no way I could be his type.

We met at Al's house to watch the NBA Championship game. That year the Miami Heat were playing the Dallas Mavericks. We talked for hours and before he left, He told me he wasn't looking for a relationship.

"I'm okay with that," I said.

I wasn't entirely sure I was telling the whole truth but I knew I wanted to stay in touch. So, 'ok' seemed like the best option. 'Ok' was enough. I got in my car and drove away. When I made it home, my phone rang and it was Noble, checking to see if I made it home safely. He told me he enjoyed my company and made it clear he wanted to see me again.

"Ok," I said. A simple two letter word to begin our saga.

That summer of 2011, Noble and I were inseparable. We were in sync, I knew when something was wrong or when he had good news to share. Wherever he was, I stood beside him and I loved it. My heart broke when he had to go back to college. As time went on, my body seemed off. My cycle still appeared, but I had food cravings and if I didn't eat what my body craved I would get sick to the stomach. When I mentioned my food cravings to my older sister, Pam, only one thing seemed like a logical explanation.

"You might be pregnant," she said.

The thought never crossed my mind and I refused to let it. The next day I visited my momma at her house and also told her about the food cravings and just like Pam she suspected I was pregnant. I was in denial and didn't want my Mom to know I was having sex.

"There's no way I can be pregnant. I'm not sexually active," I said letting the lie roll off my tongue.

I tried to hide the fear in my voice but the more the word 'pregnant' was said the more I worried. Later that evening, Noble and I talked letting him know about the alleged pregnancy. He said there was only one way to find out. So that November, after work I went to buy two pregnancy tests.

The two red lines glared back like flares signaling for rescue. This couldn't be happening. I convinced myself it was a faulty test and decided to take another, only to be proven wrong again.

I was pregnant.

"I can't have this baby," I heard myself say out loud, not fully sure if they were my own words. I was more concerned with the thoughts of others than my own, not taking my own feelings into consideration.

Noble couldn't change my mind so he didn't try, he simply agreed, leaving me with the life altering decision. Therefore, it was settled. I was going to the abortion clinic.

I prayed the pregnancy tests from home were all wrong, hoping they were simply defects with the tests. As the nurse looked onto the sonogram machine and pushed closer to my cervix, she looked at me puzzled.

"How far along do you believe you are in your pregnancy?" she asked.

I laid on the bed confused. Maybe those tests were faulty after all. I begin to smile on the inside, but as I opened my eyes her facial expressions alarmed me.

"What's wrong? Ma'am was the pregnancy tests wrong?" I said.

"No, the tests were correct. You're pregnant, but I think you are further along than you think."

"I can't be too far along, maybe a few weeks at the most," I said

"I'm sorry sweetie, you're more than a few weeks. You're about 9 weeks and 5 days."

I couldn't believe my ears. I began to break down in disbelief. How could I be this far along? I went out to the waiting room to share the news with my friend. She became ecstatic and tried to convince me to keep the child, but to no avail. I decided to go through with the abortion, not realizing later how this would haunt me. I sucked up my feelings and went to the operating room succumbing to the anesthesia that soon followed.

I woke up in my friend's bed and I felt horrible. All I could do was lay there. For two days. I did just that. As much as I wanted to forget in that moment, one question continued to revolve: Can I have my unborn child back?

Noble and I never discussed the abortion after the procedure. Instead, we tried to keep things normal. We texted and spoke on the phone throughout the day; yet, I didn't feel the same. I felt like a stranger to the guy I once knew. I wanted the baby back. I wanted Noble to express himself to me. I was upset that he was not there physically to comfort me, hold me and tell me it would be okay. He mentally checked out, leaving me to cipher through my many emotions alone.

In January, I did a twenty-one day fast with my church. Noble agreed to do the fast with me too. When the fast was over we decided to go our separate ways. I woke up and the thoughts of wanting my baby back changed. The baby was not coming back and I knew it. I wanted peace and I needed it bad, but it felt unreachable. I felt just as catastrophic as a category five tornado. I just wanted my life to pause.

Yes, I need God, but I need a therapist too!

<u>BREATHE</u>

Let me out of the box
Suffocating
I still cannot breathe
Suffocating
Every second
every moment
I'm in deep waters with no way to escape
Silence is almost worth dying for
What more do you want from me?
Suffocating
Story after story
affairs upon affairs
Person after person
I just want to breathe again
I am suffocating
Everyone depends on my thoughts,
my opinions
my advice
and all my time
Help me...
breathe

BLACK GIRLS NEED THERAPY

My mind was racing.

At the age of 25, I could not believe what was happening. I answered the phone while sitting at my desk, with Bre on the other end of the line, screaming.

Losing my mother to the prison system seemed unreal. I could not be without my mother for four years. I went from talking to her daily to only hearing her voice during visits. I would drive from Jacksonville to Ocala to see her but our visits were too short. I needed a solution to my problems fast but I didn't know where to start.

I needed some time to get away, go on a vacation, or talk to someone. I felt so off balanced. I was unsure as to what it was but every day it was as if I was painting over the imperfections which only exposed them more. I needed to scrape off the old, sand it down, buff and apply new paint. But I felt numb and I couldn't shake it. I would sleep and let time pass me by, not wanting to hear from others. I immersed my body in between the covers and vowed never to return. I quit my job working for the state as a child protective investigator because I was no good to myself and I could not effectively perform my job duties. I needed a solution, but I didn't want to seem crazy or have a label placed on me.

When my mom was convicted, I went to go visit Crystal. Crystal suggested I make an appointment to see a therapist. I told her no because people would think I was crazy. Yet as time went on and it became harder to cope I realized I was not able to manage my emotions, so I decided to seek help.

Through therapy, I discovered what I was going through. Depression is what he called it. It felt like a curse word. How and when did I allow this to happen? I did not want to be depressed and I sure did not want to add another label to the list I already had. Yet here I was, depressed and seeing a therapist.

Therapy is for white people, rich people, crazy people—people who lose their absolute mind—at least that's what I tried to convince myself. "I don't need therapy," a phrase I said to myself too many times. Paying to sit across someone on a couch while they stared and nodded and took notes on their notepad, saying things such as "that must be hard" and "how did you feel" didn't make sense to me. No, therapy was never an option—until it became my only option.

I arrived at Mr. John's office apprehensively stepping into the room. A simple dark grey couch, a bookshelf, a rug, and a Chinese evergreen which sat in the corner of the room served as his decor.

"Do I have to lay on the couch?"

"Do whatever makes you comfortable," he said.

I didn't move. I stood close to the door ready to make my exit. He walked over and took a seat on the floor, on the rug, legs crossed with no notepad in sight.

***

Fear of the unknown gripped me stronger than a choke hold. Exploring this therapy thing paralyzed me. I tried to talk myself out of therapy many times. My community was not receptive to therapy. I could not name one person with the color of my skin in my inner circle who ever expressed that going to talk to a "shrink" was an okay thing to do. Therapy was not an option so I struggled with seeking help. But when things became tougher, I gave in and started to do my research. Google was my best friend. By definition, therapy is, "treatment intended to relieve or heal a disorder or the treatment of mental or psychological disorders by psychological means." I read the definition a few times taking in every word. Therapy may not be that bad I said to myself. After more research, I realized that therapy could assist to relieve my emotions.

I googled local therapist not too sure what to look for. The one thing I did know was I had to be cautious of the person I was about to allow into my space. Should I have a female or male? Should he or she be black? Or should I try this completely blindfolded? I decided to put everything on the line.

"Hey, I'm Shanita", I said. My voice was stringent, my cover to hide the fear.

"I'm John. It's a pleasure to meet you, Shanita. What brings you in today?"

"Mr. Therapist, how will this help me get out the bed?"

"Ma'am, you will get what you put out. We must work together to understand the root cause of what you're going through. Now, what other reserves or perceptions do you have about this process?"

Like a water hose gushing with water, I asked away. "Do I have to take medication? What will be my diagnosis? Am I crazy? And can you really help me?"

Mr. John was earnest. He answered my questions one at a time and before I knew it our session was over, one hour later.

"Before you go I have a homework assignment for you and I'll see you in a couple weeks."

He handed me a journal and encouraged me to use it as I saw fit. I walked out of his office and knew that I would be back

***

Next session:
"Hey, did you bring your journal?"
"Yes."
"Okay, read it to me."

He asked me why I was against medication if I

thought I needed it and if I had to diagnose myself what would I call it. I thought maybe I needed to at least give it a try because remaining in bed was not an option.

MEDICATION MANAGEMENT

I was completely against taking medication. I watched my younger brother, Quan, take medication after being diagnosed with ADHD and I hated how it made him feel. "it makes me feel sick," he often complained. He explained taking medication would make him feel as if he was having an out of body experience. I remember a time when my aunt and I picked him up from elementary school, and he stood as still as a statue. When he got into the back of the van he sat very quietly, as if he was in a trance. Once the medicine wore off, he explained the school staff gave him too much. Seeing him in that state, altered my view of taking medication.

"Everyone reacts to medication differently, just as we are all different," Mr. John explained. He ran through the pros and cons of taking medication. Hearing from his point of view caused me to consider it. *Maybe it would help,* I thought to myself but I couldn't shake the thought of my brother. I decided not to take medication and just wanted to continue to engage in sessions, and use my coping skills and other techniques. Medicine just wasn't a choice for me.

<u>HEALING</u>

The sessions that followed continue to build on each other. I greatly appreciated Mr. John for the holistic perspective he brought to each session. He was able to relate to me in a way I did not think could exist between the black girl and the white male therapist.

<u>WAKE UP OR TURN THE PAGE</u>

1. Know your triggers.
2. Take your own advice and use it.
3. Be able to identify your likes and dislikes.
4. Trust and embrace your process.

9/5/2016

Dear Self,

Today was not a good day. I'm not sure if I can get out the bed to look at myself in the mirror and dress up. I want to just give up. There's too much going on. I feel as though every time I attempt to take a step forward, I take five steps backward which continues to put me behind. I do not understand why I am not able to just come out of this funk.

Pull yourself together, Shanita. What is truly your problem? Will you continue to blame yourself from past hurts and disappointments? I cannot seem to find my way out.

Stuck. I am drowning. This time I am not sure if I wanted help. I appear to be stuck in another body or a different world. My mind is running faster than I can keep up.

I give up....

BACK ON TRACK

The tears begin to flow.

Where did I go wrong? I need to get back on track. What does being on track look like for me? I need to get myself together. Build my credit score. Buy a home. Become successful and stable in my career. I want to meet the guy just for me and begin a family. So where do I go from here? I have to wake up or try to change the page. No longer will fear grip me or suffocate me in the puddle of the past. I am climbing out because I want to live in my purpose. I cannot go through with another abortion. Therefore, I will pick myself up, dust off and try it again.

1 CORINTHIANS 16:13-14

My current relationship with Antwoine has been a blessing, yet challenging. He caused me to become more confident in who I am. At the beginning of our relationship, he challenged me to be the best me, fully and authentically.

"This is the year Shanita meets Denise," he said. I turned and looked at him confused.

"What do you mean by that?"

"You have lived doing for others, ensuring that others around you are happy, but what makes you happy? Where is your confidence in yourself?"

I was baffled but his questions forced me to self-reflect.

The days we disagreed most were the days he challenged me about an ex I wasn't ready to let go. I would tell myself I was over him yet would become defensive at the mention of his name. This happened for some time until one day—Super Bowl Sunday 2018—I decided I had to let go if I truly desired to give Antwoine access to me.

I was afraid to allow Antwoine in my space

because I did not want to be hurt again. I knew he would eventually leave because I continued to push him away, but he stayed. He ensured me that God gave him the word needed to remain in the relationship and he wanted to make sure that he listened. He even decided to practice celibacy with me, an act no other man ever offered. I trusted him. He showed me I could. He always kept his word and worked hard to keep a smile on my face. He became my best friend and my closest confidant.

I recognized that my issue was that I'd been expecting and looking for a love that Antwoine could not give me. He can only love me in his way, out of his definition of love. This caused me to understand that it is vital for children to have both parents active in their lives. It's just as important to have a relationship with God at the center of your life to help cultivate your perceptions of love and ensure your heart and thoughts are as pure as possible. As I grow up and work to become a beautiful me, I must look in the mirror daily!

"Be on your guard; stand firm in the faith; be courageous; be strong. Do everything in love."

SHANITA MEETS DENISE

"Heal your childhood before you contaminate your adulthood" -
Kamire' Kelley

Hello Healing.
Goodbye Hurt.

Sometimes your journey is connected to others whether that be through family, friends, therapy or a combination of the three and that's a part of my story.

The idea, Shanita meets Denise was birth out of my current relationship.

Antwoine and I met during a pivotal time in my journey to self-discovery. He was graced to walk in my world and has shined lights on those dark places I worked so hard to paint over hoping the paint would blend in perfectly. He challenged me to look at the woman in the mirror no matter how much I said go away with my actions.

One day, while driving down the road, Antwoine had the nerve to say Noble played me and suggested I gave Noble too much credit. I went livid in a split of a half of a second. "Are you kidding me? You don't know what you're talking about and you don't have a right to speak on what you don't know. It wasn't like that and clearly you misunderstood what I have shared with you. Why do you feel the need to bring Noble up, it has nothing to do with you!"

Oh, shucks. Did I just snap on him about Noble? I turned to look out the window because I was too embarrassed to look at him to his face. I was supposed to be healed and ready to progress in my relationship with him yet here I was, lashing out about my ex. What triggered me to react to something as simple as a challenge for me to look at the whole picture instead of pieces I adopted to believe. In that moment, I came to understand that it's not abnormal to re-experience things and it wasn't my job to beat myself up, but to know it's okay, it's a part of the process.

I felt most vulnerable to want to continue the road of healing. Antwoine grabbed my hand and stated, "this is the year Shanita meets Denise". You will get through this. You can be all that you were purposed to be. A friend once told me, "to be happy does not mean your life is perfect. It means you understand how to respond to adversity with grace, faith, and a smile". What you have in mind can be contrary to His thoughts. Have faith in God. If you do not watch what you have in mind, it can be contaminated.

I've made progress to becoming whole. Hello Shanita, I'm Denise. It's nice to meet you. This is the discovery of me. When I introduce myself, I am eager to state my name, not just a part of my name.

In this current chapter of my life, I get over all the baggage from previous chapters to discover ME. As a social worker, I work every day to empower and assist families to see the whole picture and become acceptable to working on the whole not just a piece. I begin to take my own advice.

Where do I begin to become holistic? Me as a holistic individual makes me aware that my story is beyond me. All life experiences and lessons were to assist the next family through and lead by example in my own authenticity.

You must begin with an open mind even when things are out of your realm of knowledge and being acceptable to receive help from others. You must be willing to be comfortable with being uncomfortable. Looking in the mirror is a way for me to be accountable to self!

Get help! Talk to someone, take time to get to know yourself; have an open mind to be willing to receive, be okay with saying okay, I need help and I want to be better; how do I become a better me. Get educated because where you lack knowledge; you'll be left behind. Have a support system. You shouldn't act on the opinions of others or their perceptions about you and decisions based off religion. Therefore, I begin to redefine my faith and relationship with God myself.

You may ask what did that look like, for me I begin to journal. I put my thoughts on paper daily, read my Bible to gain understanding, pray, meditate and take long walks as I talk aloud to God. I even gave social media a break because I needed no distractions. Break the cycles and break down what happen so that you don't transition those cycles to the next generation

Gloria Steinem, "The final stage of healing is using what happens to you to help other people. That is healing in itself."

Yes, I was raised in much adversity. However, I had profound impacts that begin to shape my little world even prior to my birth.

Although life started off with a trend of adversities. Here is a bit of advice. Take those adversities and turn them into achievements.

I'm not in competition with anyone, just becoming the best version of myself! I am uniquely designed, intricately wired and purposely positioned. I realized the more I tore myself down by trying to become someone else, the longer I prolonged my journey toward purpose. I was created wonderfully! Remember who You are. Remembering your position gives opportunity to change your condition (situation, problem, mishap) to change who you are.

Be a condition changer.

ABOUT THE AUTHOR

Shanita D. Jackson is a native of Orlando, Florida. She is a mentor and enjoys to travel. Shanita is a Social Worker. She is zealous about her career and dedicated to empowering others. Shanita is a genuine supporter and goes above and beyond for others. She holds a Bachelor of Social Work from Florida Agricultural & Mechanical University.

BEYOND ME

Made in the USA
Columbia, SC
31 July 2020

14443699R00036